Searchlight
BOOKS™

What
Are Earth's
Cycles?

Investigating the

Water

Cycle

Candice Ransom

Lerner Publications ◆ Minneapolis

Content Consultant: Doug Hallum, Survey Hydrogeologist, University of Nebraska–Lincoln

Lerner Publications Company
A division of Lerner Publishing Group, Inc.
241 First Avenue North
Minneapolis, MN 55401 USA

For reading levels and more information, look up this title at www.lernerbooks.com.

Library of Congress Cataloging-in-Publication Data

Ransom, Candice F., 1952–
  Investigating the water cycle / by Candice Ransom.
   pages cm. — (Searchlight books. what are earth's cycles?)
  Includes index.
  ISBN 978-1-4677-8055-1 (lb : alk. paper) —
 ISBN 978-1-4677-8341-5 (pb : alk. paper) — ISBN 978-1-4677-8342-2 (eb pdf)
   1. Hydrologic cycle—Juvenile literature. I. Title.
  GB848.R36 2016
  551.48—dc23   2015001949

Manufactured in the United States of America
1 – VP – 7/15/15

Contents

Chapter 1

WATER, WATER EVERYWHERE

Water is all around us. It fills the oceans. It makes rivers and streams flow. It forms puddles you can splash in. Some people call Earth the water planet because water covers most of its surface.

People need water to survive. What else needs water?

Every living thing on Earth needs water. Trees, flowers, and other plants must have water to grow. All animals need water to survive. In fact, the human body is 70 percent water!

Elephants drink up to 50 gallons (189 liters) of water every day. That's about the amount of water you use to take a bath.

CLOUDS MAY LOOK FLUFFY, BUT THEY ARE MADE OF WATER.

▼

Water is not only on Earth's surface. It is also high in the air and the clouds. The ground far beneath your feet contains water too.

Three States of Water

Most people think of water as a liquid. But water exists in three states. It can be a solid, a liquid, or a gas.

If you have ever played in the snow, then you have played with solid water.

Temperature affects how water changes states. Have you ever put ice in your drink? That ice is water in its solid state.

Have you ever watched a puddle dry up on a hot day? The water is turning to its gas state, known as water vapor. Water vapor is invisible.

WATER FREEZES INTO A SOLID AT 32°F (0°C).

Soon the water in this puddle will be a gas in the air.

This water is changing from a solid state to a liquid state.

Molecules Matter

Water is made of tiny particles called molecules. When water changes its state, the molecules change too. In water's solid state, the molecules stick together. In water's liquid state, they slide around one another. Molecules in water vapor move quickly and stay apart.

Water's Continuous Journey

Water is not created or destroyed. Water constantly moves from the land and oceans, into the air, and back down again. We call this journey the water cycle.

MORE THAN 96 PERCENT OF
EARTH'S WATER IS IN THE OCEANS.

The water cycle needs two things to keep it moving. It needs Earth's gravity. It also needs energy from the sun.

The sun shines on a beautiful waterfall in Iceland.

See the Cycle

Water changes to vapor when heated to 212°F (100°C). At that temperature, water boils. But water can rise into the air without being boiled. Warmer temperatures cause it to become a vapor more quickly. You can test the effect of different temperatures on water.

Pour 2 teaspoons (10 milliliters) of water into the lid of a jar. Repeat with a second lid. Put one lid in warm sunlight. Place the second in a cooler, shady spot. Check the lids the next day. Is there less water in one lid than the other? What does this tell you about temperature's effect on water?

Chapter 2

WATER ON THE MOVE

Earth's gravity and energy from the sun drive the water cycle. Most of Earth's water is stored in the oceans. The sun warms the surface of the oceans.

Gravity is an important part of the water cycle because it pulls raindrops down to Earth. What else drives the water cycle?

This heat makes the water molecules on the ocean's surface move faster. Some molecules break away and rise into the air as water vapor. This process is called evaporation.

AFTER A WATER MOLECULE EVAPORATES, IT SPENDS ABOUT TEN DAYS IN THE AIR.

What Is Condensation?

Winds push the water vapor upward. The wind also blows particles of dust. High in the atmosphere, temperatures are cooler. Cooled water vapor bumps into dust. The water vapor clings to the surface of the dust particles. Water droplets form. This process is called condensation.

Water vapor is in the air around you. This vapor turns into droplets of liquid water when it touches a cold bottle.

See the Cycle

Place six ice cubes in a glass and leave it in the sunlight. What happens? Solid water melts into a liquid. Pour the melted water into a pan. Ask an adult to place the pan on the stove. Let the water come to a boil. Do you see wisps of mist disappearing into the air? That is evaporation in action. Ask the adult to take the pan off the stove. Put the lid on the pan. Wait a few seconds, and then remove the lid. Do you see water droplets inside the lid? Condensation can happen when water vapor touches a surface with a lower temperature.

When a cloud forms on Earth's surface, it is called fog.

All about Clouds

Condensation creates clouds. Did you know clouds are part of the water cycle? A cloud is made of billions of water droplets that float in the air. Those droplets may join with other droplets and become bigger.

Many droplets become too big and heavy to stay in the air. Because of gravity, these droplets fall back to Earth in the form of rain. If the air around the cloud is very cold, the droplets may become freezing rain, snowflakes, or hail. Water that falls from the air to Earth is called precipitation. Precipitation is necessary to continue the cycle.

STATES OF WATER

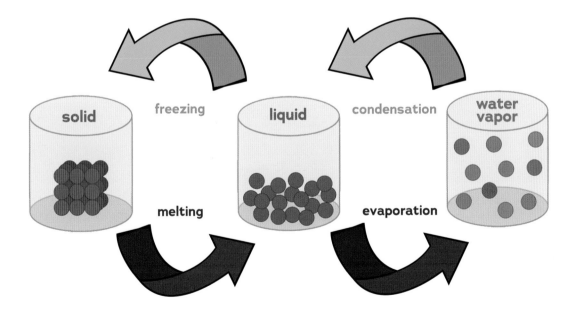

Chapter 3

SURFACE WATER

We know that most of Earth is covered by water, not land. That means most precipitation does not fall on land. Most of it falls back into the oceans. It also collects in seas, lakes, and rivers.

Some precipitation collects in rivers such as this one. Where does most precipitation fall?

Part of Earth's surface water is frozen. The North Pole is in a sea covered by floating ice. The South Pole is on a landmass coated by an ice sheet.

THE FROZEN CONTINENT AT THE BOTTOM OF EARTH IS CALLED ANTARCTICA.

Water in Glaciers

Frozen water is also in glaciers. A glacier is a large, slowly moving mass of ice. It forms when snow builds up in one place for many years and creates a thick ice mass. The ice is mixed with dirt and rocks.

GLACIERS OFTEN MOVE ABOUT
3 FEET (1 METER) PER DAY.

This glacier is slowly moving down a mountain, and it has almost reached the sea.

With time, the ice mass grows heavier and heavier. A glacier's own weight causes it to move. The force of gravity makes glaciers slide very slowly downhill.

Water in glaciers and ice caps can remain frozen for thousands of years. But this water is still part of the water cycle. Over time, warmer temperatures can cause the ice to melt. The water then flows into rivers, lakes, and oceans.

This river is formed by melted water from a glacier.

LESS THAN 3 PERCENT OF EARTH'S WATER IS FRESHWATER.

▼

Freshwater and Salt Water

The water in Earth's oceans is salty. Only a small amount of the water on Earth is fresh, or not salty. Most freshwater is frozen in the ice caps and glaciers.

Drinking salt water makes humans and animals sick. Some people do not have access to freshwater. Turning ocean water into freshwater is very costly. The process uses a lot of energy. Scientists are working on ways to make it less expensive.

EARTH'S WATER

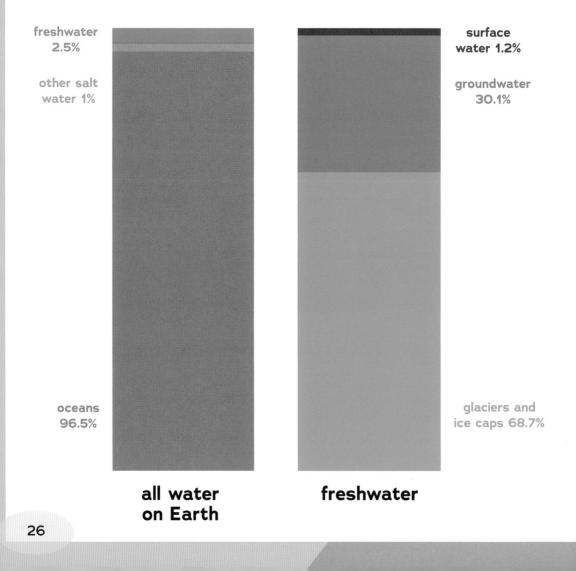

freshwater 2.5%

other salt water 1%

surface water 1.2%

groundwater 30.1%

oceans 96.5%

glaciers and ice caps 68.7%

all water on Earth

freshwater

See the Cycle

Did you know that you can make freshwater from salt water? Pour 3 cups (710 ml) of water into a large bowl. Add 1.5 tablespoons (22 ml) of salt. Stir to dissolve the salt. Place a small cup into the bowl of water. Make sure the salt water does not get into the cup. Cover the bowl with plastic wrap and seal the edges. Place a small rock above the cup in the center of the plastic wrap.

Set the bowl in the sun. After several hours, remove the plastic. Is there water in the cup? Taste it. Is it salty? The salt water evaporated in the sun and then condensed into its liquid state. The salt stayed behind in the bowl.

Chapter 4

THE WATER CYCLE ON LAND

Not all precipitation falls into the oceans. Rain, freezing rain, and snow fall on land too. Precipitation can also collect in lakes and ponds.

Rain falls into a pond. What are some other places that precipitation can collect?

Rivers and streams move water back to the oceans. Melted ice and snow flow back to the oceans in this way as well. All this excess precipitation is called runoff.

The Amazon River is the source of 20 percent of all freshwater that enters Earth's oceans.

Groundwater and Saturation

Precipitation also sinks into the ground. Plants draw some of that water into their roots. The water travels up through their stems or trunks. Tiny holes in a plant's leaves let water escape into the air. The water changes state and becomes a vapor.

Some tree roots go down more than 20 feet (6 m) below the surface.

THE RAINWATER ON THESE ROCKS WILL EVENTUALLY END UP UNDERGROUND.

Water also moves below the surface as groundwater. Groundwater trickles down through cracks and spaces in the rocks and soil. If those spaces are already filled with water, the ground is saturated. That means the ground is holding all the water it can.

What Is the Water Table?

The top of the saturated area is called the water table. If you dig a hole that fills with water, you have reached the water table. The water table may be a few feet below the surface. Or it could be hundreds of feet down.

THE WATER TABLE

unsaturated area

water table

river

saturated area

THE LEVEL OF THE WATER TABLE CAN CHANGE DEPENDING ON THE SEASON. WHEN THE WATER TABLE IS LOW, RIVERS SOMETIMES GO DRY.

Groundwater flows slowly in the area below the water table. Eventually this water meets streams and rivers. Streams and rivers are where the water table is above the surface.

Most of the freshwater that people use is found in groundwater. People drill wells to reach this water. The water is usually treated. That means workers install equipment that cleans the water so it is safe for drinking.

A well brings groundwater up to the surface.

See the Cycle

Groundwater movement is different depending on the type of soil. You can watch water flow in this simple experiment. Fill a glass container with sand. Fill another with pebbles, and fill one more with dirt. Add water to each container. How fast does water move among the grains of sand? Does it move faster through pebbles? In which container did the water reach the bottom the fastest? Record your results.

THE WATER CYCLE

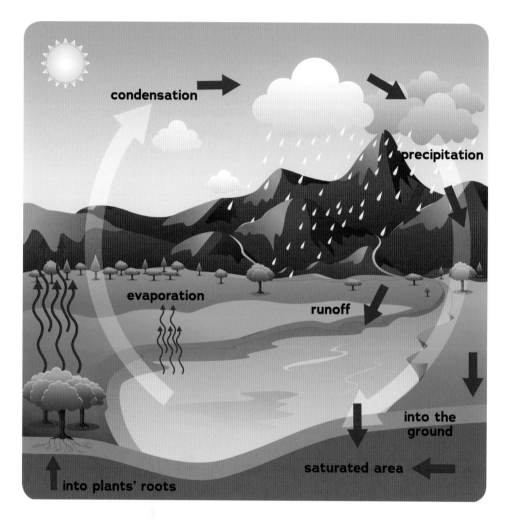

Turn on the kitchen faucet. Did any water go down the drain? If so, that water may reach a river. The river flows into the ocean. The sun shines down on the ocean. And the water cycle continues.

Science and the Water Cycle

Create your own water cycle. Place a 1-inch (2.5-centimeter) layer of pebbles in the bottom of a jar. Add a thin layer of charcoal. You can find this at pet stores. Next, add an inch of potting soil over the charcoal. Place a small plant in the jar, and cover the roots with soil. Water the plant until the soil is moist. Seal the jar with the lid.

Set the jar in a sunny window. Check it for the next few days. Write down what you observe. Do you see water droplets inside the jar lid? Water formed vapor from the leaves of your plant. That is the water cycle at work!

Glossary

condensation: the process of water vapor changing into a liquid

evaporation: the process of liquid water changing into water vapor

glacier: a large, slowly moving mass of ice. It is formed by snow and ice on mountains or in cold places.

groundwater: water held underground in the soil or in pores and cracks in rocks

molecule: the smallest possible amount of a substance, such as water

precipitation: water that falls from clouds to Earth as rain, freezing rain, snow, or hail

runoff: precipitation that does not soak into the ground or evaporate. It flows downhill into rivers and streams.

saturate: to soak or fill something to the point where no more can be absorbed

water table: the top of the saturated area belowground

water vapor: water that has changed into a gas. Water vapor is one of the three states of water.

LERNER

SOURCE

Expand learning beyond the printed book. Download free, complementary educational resources for this book from our website, www.lerneresource.com.

Learn More about the Water Cycle

Books

Fleisher, Paul. *Vapor, Rain, and Snow: The Science of Clouds and Precipitation*. Minneapolis: Lerner Publications, 2011. Learn more about the water cycle in the atmosphere and how it affects weather.

Mulder, Michelle. *Every Last Drop: Bringing Clean Water Home*. Custer, WA: Orca, 2014. This book describes the innovative ways in which people get clean water in communities around the world.

Stewart, Melissa. *Water*. Washington, DC: National Geographic, 2014. Great photography illustrates each stage in the water cycle.

Websites

Kidzone: The Water Cycle
http://www.kidzone.ws/water
This site features cool facts about the water cycle, along with fun activities.

Make a Mini Water Cycle!
http://thewaterproject.org/resources/lesson-plans/create-a-mini-water-cycle
Visit this site to create your own mini water cycle and make it rain into a mug.

The Water Cycle for Kids
http://water.usgs.gov/edu/watercycle-kids-int.html
Check out this fun-to-use interactive site that describes each step of the water cycle.

Index

Photo Acknowledgments

The images in this book are used with the permission of: © Madiz/iStockphoto, p. 4; © numxyz/iStockphoto, p. 5; © David De Lossy/Photodisc/Thinkstock, p. 6; © Ina Peters/iStock/Thinkstock, p. 7; © Valentyn Volkov/iStockphoto, p. 8; © Esteban Resendiz Reyes/FogStock/Thinkstock, p. 9; © yanikap/iStockphoto, p. 10; © Stockbyte/Thinkstock, p. 11; © Tomas Sereda/iStockphoto, p. 12; © Reece with a C/Shutterstock Images, p. 13; © Chalabala/iStockphoto, p. 14; © swongpiriyaporn/iStockphoto, p. 15; © RG-vc/iStockphoto, p. 16; © Bill Dally/iStockphoto, p. 17; © Francesco Carucci/iStock/Thinkstock, p. 18; © Arisa J./Shutterstock Images, p. 19; © Mike Pellinni/iStockphoto, p. 20; © goinyk/iStockphoto, p. 21; © Jerome Shinners/iStock/Thinkstock, p. 22; © j-wildman/iStockphoto, p. 23; © kanonsky/iStockphoto, p. 24; © shylendrahoode/iStockphoto, p. 25; © Sebalos/iStockphoto, p. 27; © TimHesterPhotography/iStock/Thinkstock, p. 28; © Andre Dib/Shutterstock Images, p. 29; © Purestock/Thinkstock, p. 30; © RayPhotographer/Shutterstock Images, p. 31; © Melissa Held/Shutterstock Images, p. 32; © gkuna/Shutterstock Images, p. 33; © Voyagerix/iStockphoto, p. 34; © fieldwork/iStockphoto, p. 35; © stockshoppe/Shutterstock Images, p. 36; © Chris Hendrickson/Masterfile/Corbis, p. 37.

Front cover: © StudioSmart/Shutterstock.com.

Main body text set in Adrianna Regular 14/20.
Typeface provided by Chank.